# THE SILVERING

**Maura Dooley** was born in Truro, grew up in Bristol, worked for some years in Yorkshire, and has lived in London for the past 25 years. She is a freelance writer and lectures at Goldsmiths, University of London. She edited *Making for Planet Alice: New Women Poets* (1997) and *The Honey Gatherers: A Book of Love Poems* (2002) for Bloodaxe, and *How Novelists Work* (2000) for Seren.

Her selection, *Sound Barrier: Poems 1982-2002*, was published by Bloodaxe in 2002, drawing on collections including *Explaining Magnetism* (1991) and *Kissing a Bone* (1996), both Poetry Book Society Recommendations. *Kissing a Bone* and her later collection *Life Under Water*, a Poetry Book Society Recommendation in 2008, were both shortlisted for the T.S. Eliot Prize. She has twice had poems shortlisted for the Forward Prize for Best Single Poem, most recently 'Cleaning Jim Dine's Heart' in 2015, a poem included in her latest collection, *The Silvering* (2016), a Poetry Book Society Recommendation.

# MAURA DOOLEY

# The Silvering

## BLOODAXE BOOKS

ISBN: 978 1 78037 094 1

First published 2016 by
Bloodaxe Books Ltd,
Eastburn,
South Park,
Hexham,
Northumberland NE46 1BS.

www.bloodaxebooks.com
For further information about Bloodaxe titles
please visit our website or write to
the above address for a catalogue.

Supported using public funding by
**ARTS COUNCIL
ENGLAND**

Cover design: Neil Astley & Pamela Robertson-Pearce.

Printed in Great Britain by Bell & Bain Limited, Glasgow, Scotland, on
acid-free paper sourced from mills with FSC chain of custody certification.

*For my family*
*– near and far.*

# ACKNOWLEDGEMENTS

Some of these poems, or versions of these poems, were published previously in: *The Guardian, The Times Higher Educational Supplement, The Independent, The Liner, Magma, New Welsh Review, The North, NYCBigCityLit, Ploughshares* (USA), *Poetry Daily, Poetry London, Poetry Review* and *The Same*, and others commissioned by the British Council/NAWE (*Climate Change*, ed. Paul Munden), the Laurence Sterne Trust (Patrick Wildgust), Goldsmiths (Michael Simpson), the Victoria & Albert Museum (*26 Treasures*, ed. John Simmons), Dulwich Picture Gallery (Kate Miller), Faber (*Jubilee Lines*, ed. Carol Ann Duffy), the Geological Society (*Map*, ed. Michael McKimm), Two Rivers Press (*A Mutual Friend: Poems for Charles Dickens*, ed. Peter Robinson; *The Arts of Peace*, ed. Peter Robinson & Adrian Blamires) and Unbound (*First Light*, ed. Erica Wagner). My sincere thanks to the friends who kept asking.

# CONTENTS

In my room, the world is beyond my understanding;
But when I walk I see that it consists of three or four hills and a cloud.

WALLACE STEVENS, 'Of the Surface of Things'

# Cleaning Jim Dine's Heart

In the afternoon sunlight at deCordova sculpture park
she is on the top rung of a pair of steps cleaning a big
dark heart. And it has everything in it, this heart. Twice.
Even the coffee pot I brought back in hand luggage
that time, when such a thing was exotic, exciting,
more or less unknown. The coffee pot that blew up, in the end,
leaving its mark on the ceiling of Oakmead Road. That one.
Here it is, unthought of, unremembered, treacly, right here
in Jim Dine's big dark heart, which needs cleaning now,
front and back. Twice. Along with all its other secrets,
writ large, packed tight, here, in sunlight. His histories.
Which are our histories, some of them at least,
hands moving in darkness, worn out shoes, rope,
the hammers and saws of a life together, coffee.
Caught forever here in a heartbeat and wiped clean now,
restored in afternoon sunlight, the darkness shining, made good.

## Sendai, City of Trees

He turns the small corner of paper
over and in, in again and smaller.
A Christmas guest, far from home, entertaining
our small girl and thinking of his baby brother
as he folds and folds.
         When we see him next
his pale, sad, face will fill the screen, his English,
Best-in-Town, will speak of how families
have disappeared, whole streets have folded
in upon themselves, again and smaller.

But for now, he opens his palms and smiles,
a perfect crane stands ready, my daughter
claps her hands and in that moment
he makes the delicate ancient bird both sing and fly.

## Still Life with Sea Pinks and High Tide

Thrift grows tenacious at the tide's reach.
What is that reach when the water
is rising, rising?

Our melting, shifting, liquid world won't wait
for manifesto or mandate, each
warning a reckoning.

Ice in our gin or vodka chirrups and squeaks
dissolving in the hot, still air
of talking, talking.

# Complaint

You never write, they said,
the story of our lives,
the fish who bore the mark
of feline teeth, who gasped
behind the desk, till saved
by Dad, who swam alone,
so sad, the fish who swam alone.

You never write, they said,
the story of the colour flash
that filtered through our days,
asked nothing but the flakes
of crumbs we threw, the flicker
that became the cat's TV,
the glint that grew ungainly
in his tank, the steadfast eye,
the solemn mouth, the constancy.

You never write, they said,
of here and now, the lives we live,
the glint, the steadfast eye, the constant.

# The Forest at Tooting Common

Wild as any zoo,
this Common is our forest.

Scattering crumbs
you begin to walk

away from me,

here's where you learnt
you could outrun the Bogeyman

that a fox is not a wolf,

here's where you discovered
what Home might mean.

## West

Seen from the train a field like that
could take your breath away.

Not just the incline that would test
a gymfit hamstring but the ringing green of it,

the singing, ringing green you can't put a name to,
though you try, you can't put a name to

(compass interference)

the mixture of grasses and water and light glancing
that gives it that particular hue, that field,

those meadow grasses, this mild wet spring,
a field like that, seen from the train.

# Treasure Island

*(for William Smith and the bicentenary of his first geological map of England and Wales, 1815)*

> There were several additions of a later date […] and in a
> small, neat hand […] these words: *Bulk of treasure here.*
>
> ROBERT LOUIS STEVENSON

Like skinning a rabbit,
revealed beneath the old familiar
form is the raw shock of shape,
rude shades of life,
a startling blue and rose
and the creamy ochre of a jutting,
jagged backbone exposed
with everything falling from it
to the softer limbs of valley, marsh, meadow
or the naked blades of upland, scarp and moor.

Like oil on a puddle,
both muted and glinting,
the colours have settled now
and no matter the bleach and batter
of sunlight, damp, the slow turning of years,
paper folding in on itself in awkward formation,
what's charted here in new translation
is the perfect record of Truth's imagination.

# Red Rab

Not in tooth
and claw,

nor a planet's
shift of iron oxide,

not the coolest star,

neither robin, cherry,
nor the flit of fox,

not valerian
nor creeping campion,

not even
Hugh O'Neill

but mudstone, siltstone,
limestone, shale,

dear old red.

# Grotto

Shell-spangled
with the crusty shadow of death,

undergrowth
        spliced and wired
to make a bower,
reined in,
        espaliered wilderness,
crown of thorns,
          empty chamber,

through which a wind sighs
like the long withdrawing sea.

# Keen as are the arrows

If the Sky falls we shall have Larks: but who
will catch them?


A snatch of you
on Classic FM,
a smile at the thought
of your tumbling flight,
your something song
precisely caught.
I bring to it all I know
of the South Downs
killing fields,
thirty-thousand birds a day,
netted and sent to France,
how, after that War,
we lost the taste for Lark pie.
I bring to it all I know
of late spring in Gower,
on my back, on heather,
the day marked forever
by the sudden terror
of low flyers
rehearsing for Iraq,
while something else
waited to be heard
before falling most precisely
through its own sweet song.

# And Afterwards

In the taxi from Easingwold he tells me
that the early starts and late nights don't matter,
it's a pattern he is used to, being a farmer,
*having been a farmer*, and coming into Coxwold
he tells me how on his deathbed the old man,
Christopher Thornton, gave him a pair of boots
with blades and told him how in 1919 he'd skated,
the whole village had skated, grace of Lady Wombwell,
on Newburgh pond. Ice so thick had never come again.
*If it should*, he'd said, *make sure you make good use of these.*

So when we pass the pond he slows the car,
as in a cortège, and we look out across its flat mild
stillness, where only a swan is circling now,
and then move on to where my friends will tell me
how Laurence Sterne, once vicar of Stillington,
fell through the ice, skating, how no one stirred
to help him and I wonder what it all adds up to: the ice,
the pond the gentry calls a lake, the waiting blades, all this telling.

# Melancholia

A country perhaps?
Colourless depth on three sides
and at the fourth a fence of ice
in the bosky green of five in the morning,
where the frond of a fern
                              oldest survivor
imprint left in the deepest cast of coal
comes through            despite everything,
unfurling from its fist of grief
                    a shining new tongue.

# Habit

She used to say
*better to be at the pub*
*thinking of church*
*than at church*
*thinking of the pub*

but now he thinks
he'd rather be
with those who stand
beyond the gates
of either,

murmurers
in cold and rain,
striking
a small light,

witnesses
to the slow trail of smoke:
an incense
dispersing quietly
above and all around.

## The Smoke

They watch moss greening
the damp sills opposite.

Inside a woollen keeps warm
the shoulders of a chair.

They know the news in every
office, their telltale breath

is a word in your ear.

They note, with disinterest
cracks in the block widening,

this bright, yellowing,
knot of humanity.

When Rome burns
they will be first to know.

## *A sunset touch*

A fancy from a flower bell, some one's death,
A chorus ending from Euripides, –
And that's enough for fifty hopes and fears
As old and new at once as nature's self,
To rap and knock and enter in our soul,
Take hands and dance there

ROBERT BROWNING,
'Bishop Blougram's Apology'


In the held breath of high June
when the song of the lark and children
calling is the music of the lanes,

and sheep at the estuary crop vetch,
tiptoeing on bog rippled with dusk,
step out of your life a moment

into this evening's seed-strewn breezes,
where the shift and swerve of river and sea
throws up a shape of happiness

you once knew, or didn't, or read about,
or lived out and shiver
in a sudden draught of autumn.

## Then

The party we both skipped,
so never met,
the plays we saw alone,
years in which we swam
over and under

never breaking surface,
slippy with youth, one kiss
an island between two deeps,
the birds wheeling, a fish leaping,
there, in the Before.

# Late Snow

*(6th April 2008)*

I try not to see it as meaningful,
how the flakes fall swiftly
but do not settle,
not on the roads and paths,
nor *generally all over*
but here, just here,
where an arc of forsythia bows
under this fresh, surprising weight.

Calling from another place,
you asked me once to name
the brilliant bush in your new garden
describing it, in that way of yours,
so that I saw the startling blueness of it,
the unfurling leaf and tender stem
and could say confidently, *ceonothus*,
the bush that today, years on,
in my own garden and just about to bloom,
takes on a coat of ice.

What now can I name with certainty?
The snowflakes grow larger, heavier.
Is this then, real?

## The Gift

Not long after, I lost it.
Loveliest of things,
                    hand-stitched,
so soft and subtle I barely knew it was there.

Ask me now
and though I could tell you
                    just when and where first I saw
it,
how it became essential is hard
                    and how it slipped from me,
harder still.

A last moment of neglect
or something slower,
                    more insidious,
the way, warp and weft,
a face, a voice, is sewn right in.
It was possession made me careless.

# Threnody

A wave works a difficult shore,
to the sob of pebbles
shifting, shifting,
                    at spring tide, neap tide,
slack water – that moment
before the breath draws in –
                    this moment, now,
in, in,
        till the lung aches.

## Rest

and when heat
left her need

sleep came,
ocean deep,

inviolable
unfolding leaf
of dream.

# In a dream she meets him again

The trees shake their leaves
in this loveliest of springs
lit from within, like the face
of the boy whose fresh glance
finds hers as he tilts a glass
at a book or film, at life itself,
where they sit by the river
in the red and gold of dusk
while bubbles rise to the rim,
o, o, she almost had his name.
Remember me? Maybe she does.

# In a dream she encounters a snag

A rough edge, all of a sudden,
catches like a burr and nothing
now can blunt the feel of it.

She needs his old matchbox,
the rasp of its unfunny joke,
a battered flag unfurling as she

rubs her finger nail against
the grain, gives a dust of herself
to all that is uneasy, uncertain.

# In a dream he is still busy

Finding him, in an unfamiliar room,
she sees he is with someone,
is asked to wait and waiting falls
on her like rain, a fine mist, a softness
she finds words for, *haar*, *smirr*,
stupid poetry words – till it falls harder,
faster, relentless now, streaming over
her chilled face till she can no longer see him,
he is blurred, rubbed away,
and none of those soft damp words will do
for the drowned, scoured, washed-out
loneliness of waking.

## He buys her a hot whiskey

Of all the things
he might have done
to make her feel
it was no dream,
a glowing glass,
the room's interest
molten in it,
his sense of audience
intact: this was it.

# Hurt

What do you call the place
in a tree where damage collects?
A bole blackened by disease, neglect,
a stoop pooling the slow drip
of darkened leaf,
                        the brilliance
of lightning bringing only regret
at what's been broken, torn or blasted.
What do you call that place? I forget.

# Bellowhead

There is punk, reggae,
even a moment of Masekela trumpet
but mostly the forests and woods
come walking, walking into the room

and blow, winds, and crack your cheeks
is that land, from the crow's nest,

true love neath the rose bower

and the poor man out sowing barley
or digging, digging?

Fox is a redgolden thread through
the copse, walking, walking
                              out of vellum
and crackling to life,
                              fire sparking,
moon soft under cloud, a child's cry,
an owl's sob for the drunkard in the gutter,

there's rosemary, too, that's for remembrance,
yes, and rowan

but mostly it's the bent backs working,
deep forests walking, a history of yearning.

# Setting the Moth Trap

*Eclipse*

A summer garden's
slender brindle, gold spangle,
heart and dart, prominent.


*Green Carpet*

Moss-coloured, moss-stitched,
this might be Limerick in
Nineteen Twenty-one.


*Late Summer*

One of the pleasures
in trapping Mottled Beauty
lies in its release.


*Sandy Carpet*

A cockleshell wing
opens like the memory
of a seaside town.


*The Feathered Gothic*

Wings closed in dark prayer,
the Minster's Great West window
filigree of light.

## Casey, Cullen, Ward and McKeogh, 2016

Here on the edge, he knew the early years
were best laid to rest, along with now
a row of headstones he'd flown home for.

Casey always there in his one good suit,
Ward a word they never chanced between them,
McKeogh, a rumour,

a star that rose on a sodium street.
Didn't he build the Millennium Dome?
Was he not the man behind the Montevetro?

*You'll visit now, won't you?* and Casey promises,
watching the plane head off across the Atlantic,
releasing the handbrake, nosing slowly home.

## That Old Story

The way I heard it,
it might have been a cow
or three magic beans
that kept him at market,
brought him home happy,
but she caught him smiling
and guessed it was another.
So when he threw his jacket
at the arms of a chair
she stole a look
and angry to find a picture
of some old woman, hard-looking,
mean, the very spit, in fact,
of her own mother, asked
'Why ever d'you carry this?'
and he, shyly, leant over
to show her, fondly,
his treasured find,
a very likeness of his dear old Dad.

# Life and Land, Thursday May 3rd 1979

Now Voyager sail thou forth to seek and find.

WALT WHITMAN


A spaceship spun a course from star to star,
netting Jupiter, to send home the fabulous,
a gossamer of gas dusting all the front pages,
as, far below, a Raleigh Olympus
slipped down the morning lane, scythed
the long grass, turned on the face of a daisy
to trim the edge of the Selby coalfield
whose hedges brimmed and frothed with blackthorn,
still frosty, meshed in web and filament.
General Election, first vote, maiden voyage,
and who should have been surprised
once marks were made and papers counted,
to feel that May a sudden snatch of snow
seen not as warning then but as wonder,
not as presentiment but as just a snatch of snow?
So that young face, lifted up to ice and sunshine,
still steady under the eternal shifting heavens,
turned her wheels for home, and spun out a story
from lane, hedgerow, from the day itself.

# Grass, Thursday May 7th 2015

Now Voyager depart, (much, much for thee is yet in store,)

WALT WHITMAN

The dirt beneath your feet?
You stand on it, grind it underheel,
you spit on it.

The dirt beneath your feet?
It carries seed, it nourishes,
it rises green.

# The Tooting Common Olympics

Korf Ball, Cricket and Keepie-Uppies,
Five-a-Side after work, Under-Tens on Sundays,
Tai-Chi, Frisbee, Tag Rugby, Hide and Seek,
Tennis, Yoga, Power walks twice a week,
Hockey, Hurling, Hula Hoop and Hopscotch,
runners whose desire paths rub a track through dust,
the rainbow doors of England's largest lido
open on the cool, blue-domed cathedral
of Tooting Common's field of dreams and passion,
first steps, first drink, first kiss, first walking-stick,
where still we pause beneath the oak and ash
to feel Persephone stir as leaves unfold,
or see Zeus turn the day from bronze to gold.

# At Streatham Hill Station

My daughter waits opposite
on the Up platform. A going-nowhere
train stops between us and in the time
it takes to pause and shift she's first
hidden from me, then gone.

It's true there have been too many
partings this year, too much sorrow,
but what her vanishing trick reveals
is the empty platform, on which,
not even dust has had time to settle.

## My Heart and My Liver

Magwitch, *Great Expectations*, Chapter One

Marsh gas, smoke, slant rain from the East
rattles a pattern of print onto paper,
sweeps the river to flux, an eel of a story that
opens London like a book, terror and promise
there in the *small bundle of shivers*
which made me, a child, fear the very same he
who might softly creep and creep his way
and tear me open, or that very same he
who was lamed by stones, cut by flints,
stung by nettles, the very same way
this reader now, grown, awoken, gazing
at the marsh, *just a long black horizontal line*
and the river *just another horizontal line*
feels all those words, line upon line,
enter a grateful, hungry, unreconciled heart.

# The Conversation of Thom Gunn

Before I knew the work I liked the name,
the double 'n', the 'h', and then I liked
a cool that somehow was, (how was that?)
both dangerous and English; the boys, the bars,
the sex, the San Francisco of it all,
the what it meant to be and then the loss,
the making plain, love finally, then loss again.
Now, I like the way he throws me a line,
lucid, lived-in, his spine leaning against my wall,
catching my eye, his many lives all mine.

# – go, in the form of a bird

I'm up here and down there, thought Alison. Which is me?
Am I the reflection in the window of me down there?

ALAN GARNER
*The Owl Service*, ch. 15


I glimpse her sometimes,
the girl whose face was made of flowers.

Summertime without school,
days shook their wings,
*and the room was full of petals.*

In search of mystery
I emptied the dresser of
Aynsley, Willow, Burleigh,
too familiar to be magical,
Doulton, a garland of blooms:
none of them right.

On scraps of paper
the transferred patterns of
*broom, meadowsweet, flowers of the oak,*
were a flutter of shreds
caught and coloured,
concentration, incantation,
breath and a wish for breath
for change, for transformation.

Summertime without school
*and petals, flowers falling.*
Today, my daughters, growing,
are a sweet absence in the house,
*and all about them a fragrance,*
tawny shriek of girlhood,
flight of silverbrown feathers,
rumpled bedclothes, a swinging door,
the trace of something efflorescent in the air.

Daughters in Summertime,
their faces fresh as may blossom.

Summertime without school
my days were fullempty
not knowing then what I waited for

– the feathers to scatter,
and petals to fall like breadcrumbs
as I made my way through the forest.

# From the Album

*At Cliveden*


He stands a little apart.
Box hedge and winter pansy
frames a flare of, um,
something forgotten, 1980s-vivid,
the river throws a plume
of mist and the picture slides
into blankness which might be
where he is now, quiet, a little apart,
just a stone's throw away from us.

# From the Album

*A parting glass*


and when they sat together,
the older brother and the younger,
without the landmass of the others,
the busy harbour and the open field,
there was a feeling like the welling
of a shoal of fish about to surface,
about to flash their shining selves
or snatch the air, a promise
that was fluid, solid, here and now

# From the Album
*i.m. fh 1943*


Here's another, the last he sent.
A young girl leans against ivy and brick,
her violin glints like a shield to the dark.
*His* girl. Serious.
The one who wrote so nicely
to your Ma, after the telegram.
No one now recalls her name,
nor if she called her violin a fiddle,
nor what the leafy wall kept in or out.

# From the Album

*The missing*

When did you become
the longago?

Run to me, run to me,
with all your news,

so that I may watch
that tiny, flickering pulse,

beating, beating, beating.

# Mr Kington's Sidecar

parked at an angle outside,
or, come to think of it, not his
but Uncle Barney's, courtesy uncle,
who called in most mornings for tea with Mrs K.
Uncle Barney's gleaming bike and sidecar
gingerly mounted by Mrs K, admired by Mr K
(who had a van), desired by me,
till the row nextdoor that is. Dad laughed
but windows trembled as doors slammed,
after which, no one saw the sidecar again,
nor the gleaming bike, nor the courtesy uncle.
I turned my gaze to the boy across the road.

# Volver

If fire threw its shape
across the wall,
your shadow licked into its heart,
a draft from the open door
might flush a shower of sparks
into the night,
a shower of sparkling light.
If fire threw its shape
against the wall,
the thought of you caught
for that moment, incandescent,
burning bright, might,
just for that moment, slip from me
and I, turning from this room
might close that door, tight.

## Revenant

In the train, in the dim glass,
you, long dead, slip your face
over mine. A mask, a shade, a past
that is somewhere there, in the dark
but not here, nor in any other scored-out
street my dog-eared notebook holds,
not here, your voice gone, your name
held in a fold of paper in a pocket,
nor here, where our eyes meet.

## Mirror

In my mother's house
is the friendly mirror,
the only glass in which I look
and think I see myself,
think, yes, that's what
I think I'm like,
that's who I am. The only
glass in which I look and smile.

Just as this baby smiles
at the baby who always
smiles at her, the one in
her mother's arms, the mother
who looks like me, who
smiles at herself in her
mother's mirror, the friendly
mirror in her mother's house.

But if I move to one side
we vanish, the woman I thought
was me, the baby making friends
with herself, we move to one side
and the mirror holds no future, no past,
in its liquid frame, only the corner
of an open window, a bee visiting
the ready flowers of summer.

# The Gough Looking-glass

*In the British Galleries, Victoria & Albert Museum*


The notes suggest it's all about this frame;
Plague, Restoration, London frosts or flame,
gesso, paint, glaze, specks of gilt and varnish,
silver leaf that turns each day to tarnish.

I think within is where the spirit dwells.
Whose face dipped in this pool to glimpse herself?
What shadow slipped through that straight gate as cloud?
Memento mori, hour glass, Turin shroud.

## Siglo de Oro

The shadows throw back gleams,
slivers of memory caught
in the silvering.
                    Is this why
when the moment comes
we open a window, shroud
even the mirrors?
                    Is this why
Buendia's dream of glass or ice
would only ever raise a past,
the future dissolving into brilliance?

## *Three Rooms,* 1937

*Paul Nash (Tate Gallery)*


Not rooms I'd ever know
but she may have,
I think,
a redblue uncertainty
of sunset, high tide,
*the gathering storm,*
waits beyond
the open door
that led her in,
the closed door
that held her there.

## Climate Change

The weather in my mother's house is misty.

Sometimes still the Freeze of '63,
when she slipped through the loft hatch,
as Persephone rising, gathering snow
before it could print dampness
on the waiting house below.

From time to time it is the fog of '65,
when hidden faces are suddenly, shockingly,
there. How they run at her,
vivid now, too close and frowning,
or saying something cloudy.

But it is never the searing summer of '76,
the season I first fell in love.
She does not recall
the slick of sweat at its heart,
its tender, tinder verges.

More often it is the winter of '47,
the face of the land first stony, then awash,
as if nothing would ever come right again.
To have lived through so much, so much,
to find first ice, then mud.

# Professor

'Where' they call 'are your great works?'

GILLIAN CLARKE,
'Letter from a Far Country'


Since you ask, they're here, in this small bedroom.
Each folded sheet a cotton one
with footnotes, endnotes,
yellow with the years. Each file a phial.
Every day a new test.
You are suspicious of such scholarship?
How may it prove useful or profound?
I'll have you know this research
is vast as any wardrobe, hot as a bath,
tight as a bandage. This knowledge
is tender as memory itself, large as life.
I am learning it by heart.
I am learning what Death may look like.

Watch and wait.
Consider the dust sparkles,
how many they are, how various.

There are several ways to study.
This bedroom is my university now.
Hand me my gown!

## So few and such morning songs

DYLAN THOMAS: 'Fern Hill'

*(for Mary Dooley)*


Are these the ferns that curled at every step,
that blackened the brackish puddles and slippery stones
filtering to green the dark and smoky days,
as your paths crossed on the morning walk to school?

The sea was teeming then with coal and ore,
the sky a steamy blur that you took in,
clambering up the steps and over the hill
staring out at the rippling blue beyond. Out.

He returned to name the names
of gone-shops, gone-pubs, gone-streets:
where change would anyhow have robbed,
rubbed out, rid the uncley alleys of the family face
if War itself had not made dust of the hardware of youth.

You returned long after he was gone to see the hill
uncoil again each spring, the waves pull in their net
of scrap and spoil, cockles and weed, rope and oil,
a lonely sea mine loosened from the depths,
the charge alive and singing in its rusty chains.

# Littoral

That winterspring, mother, the land wept for you.
The meadows blossomed with swans

the bridges floated or were swept away
I one side, you the other.

This season, the Levels are sluiced,
crossings restored, rhines hold their shape,

though now the familiar coastline is smudged,
and here in London rain floods the streets.

# Vanitas

*In ictu occuli*

Up, up through the house
as if childhood itself had fallen
long ago down the old stairwell
and back came not treacle
nor the echo of a splash,

spooling unspooling,

but the murmur of lives lived,
a shuffle of bags, shoes and coats,
the shudder and slap of mail on mat,
the smell of toast, a distant voice asking

*is the fire lit yet?*

and the door opening and closing
and opening onto icy flags, shouting,
a scent of roses, laughter, darkness.